THE QUIET WORLD

Poems by Trëndafile Visha

Transcendent Zero Press

Houston, Texas

Copyright © 2018 Trëndafile Visha.

PUBLISHED BY TRANSCENDENT ZERO PRESS
www.transcendentzeropress.org

All rights reserved. No part or parts of this book may be reproduced in any format whether electronic or in print except as brief portions used in reviews, without the expressed written consent of Transcendent Zero Press, or of the author Trëndafile Visha.

ISBN-13: 978-1-946460-06-6

Printed in the United States of America

Transcendent Zero Press
16429 El Camino Real Apt. 7
Houston, TX 77062

Cover design by Glynn Monroe Irby

Cover image taken from https://pxhere.com/en/photo/489329

THE QUIET WORLD

Poems by Trëndafile Visha

BOOK REVIEW ON TRËNDAFILE VISHA'S VALUABLE POETRY PROSE

By: Alisa Velaj

On literary interpretations that we encounter, almost always, we refer to statements that authors make for their own 'creations'. The very same feeling happens to me every time I make an effort to reflect on the poetical prose of Trëndafile Visha, an Albanian writer who compiled stories some time ago in her book: "The Same Fate in 100 Travels". "As it appears we are crazy about that little light amid obscurity," writes Visha, in a dialogue, from one of her poetical prose. This sentence is as valuable as a magic key used to discover many of the messages that Trëndafile Visha is transcending in her literary work, which reveals a sort of literary text, based on its genre that is not explored in depth so far in Albanian literature. It is a poetical prose, were in only a paragraph, or two paragraphs (there are rare prose volumes where their texts are longer than this one) the author encompasses a wide array of meditations. All of these living pieces aspire to discover that light at the middle of obscurity, but due to one reason or another, the lyrical subject, or subjects sitting in a shadow, are unable to find such a light, or briefly encounter that light and loose it again.

"And I am not obscurity. Not a dog. I am one of you, sitting at my home's entrance looking at the world being destroyed. Years ago I thought about the oak tree. Was thinking of sitting down on its shadow. But now, it is getting burned. And I cannot understand, whether above its ashes flowers will grow again. Whether kids will be born again. Whether a man will be a man again. And a woman would be a woman. Among bodies, souls, and pure love. Dogs' longing is terrible. It is terrible, that silence..."

This poetical prose transcends from top to bottom by a dark humor, almost the same as the miniature texts of Russian writer Daniil Kharms. The contemporary tenets, based on the dark humor of literature and drama, are referred to a combination of a feeling of longing and that of grotesque, with humor and farces. Such a combination takes the reader to worrisome effects, absurdity and miseries of life. The reader of Visha's prose is endlessly worried from the same fate that awaits him as a final result even though a journey's starting point is projected on diverse directions that are not similar to one another. The fate of all lyrical subjects' journeys and of shadow characters (because they never get the spotlight, independently of their chaotic attitude to reach such a stage) is at the end a humiliating fate, with the only existing path of obscurity. All of the attempts reveal the meanings along the ways of absurdity and misery that are flourishing as the only evil plant.

The lyrical subject openly accepts that he is made to smile, since at the end of the day he does not accomplish even the elementary processes; that of embodiment of a certain being. This subject is not darkness nor a dog, but a George Zamza that wakes up every morning, at a state between man and animal. At the prose of Visha, man is made into an animal due to the desire of others and himself. Just like in the texts of Franz Kafka, the subject judges others and makes his own judgment. And more surprisingly, just like in court, and in self conclusion, he has a surprising lucidity. Enliven his mind that is unable to detach him from the darkness where he is engulfed.

The subject and characters in the shadow are unable to be free from the handcuffs of obscurity, are unable to be an oak tree. The symbol of Oak as a metaphor for sustainability and life continuity, appears repeatedly in the poetical prose, the very same way as in the poetry of the author, but not to unravel the image of Jeronim De Rada in his famous verse of "MIlosao": "Life had changed many oaks", but to give a eulogy for all those sitting under the oak's shadow, after an absurd thunderstorm, that travels to our timeless existentialism.

When we read a text that develops a value over a spiritual experience and includes a spiritual perception from the act of reading, then is born a spiritual experience inside ourselves. (Stan Scott, 'Poetry and the Art of Meditation: Going behind the Symbols,' p.77). Everything is covered within the poetical prose "The same fate in 100 travels" are spiritual experiences juxtaposed in a way of a palimpsest memory, where every layer of thought reveals a dynamic of thinking not only comical but also tragic, while that dark humor is shaped in a perfect way by its author. Such a dark humor is the same with the one that is revealed by Daniil Kharms, where the characters repeat the same action over and over and are unable to accomplish what they start. Let's take a look at one of his excerpts in order to shed more light on our comparison between Trëndafile Visha and the Russian Literature Giant, while referring to one of his typical prose in this field.

"An old woman, from an infinite curiosity jumped from the window, fell down and was made into pieces. On another window, came out another old woman who was watching her neighbor crushed on the sidewalk, but from her exhilaration even she decided to jump, and turned into pieces. Then the third old women jumped from the window, then the fourth and the fifth... But when the sixth old lady jumped from the window, I detested this grim scenario and decided to visit Malcjevskij's Bazaar, where they say that a blind gentlemen received a handmade scarf as a gift. (Daniil Kharms, "The fall of old ladies", translated into Albanian by Agron Tufa).

So the characters of Visha are always led by a tragic fate, a trip through dead ends. They fall and fall within the very same net just like the old women of Kharms. But different to the Russian author, where is revealed the whole tragic scenario through epic situations and is the author that reveals the events of other personages; in our author's epics and lyricism it is dissolved as one. The author is extending over herself and others, while not detaching the lyrical self from her beings. The style of Visha comes from a telegraphic sentence, very intense, where memory is folded and is headed towards palimpsest messages. The reading of poetical prose starts exactly at the moment where we have just finished reading with one single breath. If we look at Umberto Eco, the inter-textual irony sheds light in this first detracted imagination of being an absolute attraction, expects discoveries for all those that have lost the meaning of transcendentalism. (Umberto Eco, on Literature, by Donika Omari, Tirana 2007, p. 226). The irony in the prose of Visha reaches the level of grotesque, where smile is only shaped among the readers' lips, since only an instant afterwards, he feels the eruption of joy and absurdity in his soul, because at the end of it, there is time to smile and even less time to cry, at the night that emerges as the only day and is getting married without any witnesses...

"Today was married without a witness. No one saw the groom on her side. With the exception of a door lock, at the great gate in a

City Hall. And Church did not open the doors. In a Mosque, worshipers were praying on their own. And the bride, very old, swore to the unknown somewhere else. Tomorrow, according to customs, bed sheets will be hanging on the fence. And humankind, just like human kind wait (when they have nothing else to do) perhaps one would say that the day was a virgin?!'

Visha exposes finally a sort of literary text that we hope it becomes a solid tradition in our literature, to express a myriad of lights and shadows of human soul in other literary dimensions.

Translated from Albanian Language: Peter M. Tase (Milwaukee, WI)

A daylight was married without any witness. No-one saw the groom on her side. With an exception of a lock, at the Great Entrance of City Hall. And the church did not open its doors. On a Mosque, worshipers were praying on their own. And the bride, very old was investing loyalty with the unknown somewhere else. Tomorrow, according to tradition, bed sheets will be extended on the fence. And people, are waiting as usual (when the have nothing else to do) Wouldn't you think that the Daylight would have been a virgin?

...

We smiled when lighting was in the sky. We remained silent when they descended above others. As if we would not be there. Now that they are exploding at the corner of the garden, we are shaking. And we ask, without waiting for an answer, why the time brings a thunderstorm. Prayers were dissolved. We simply wait. An unusual departure. As a crowd, crossed over a pyramid of wood logs that we built for ourselves. Wasn't the neighbors dog barking sometime ago? And we were stating, our wishes to family members of the one who is gone. We followed funerals. Expressed improvised words at the moment for all deceased. Without feeling and experiencing death. We waited for it's large impact.

...

There it comes. Dogs are barking in a crowd with their heads up and feel scratching the soil. We don't even have time to prepare for farewell. For the kids that don't know anything, why is the dog screaming. And we will not be able to keep in our chest when we leave. We will not be able to beg a pardon.
And I am not obscurity. Not a dog. I am one like you, sitting at a home entrance while looking at the world falling backwards. Some time ago I was thinking of the red oak tree. I said I would be taking a break there. But now, even this tall tree was burning. And I cannot find out, that above its ashes a flower will grow again. if a baby will be born again. If a man would become a man. And a women, would be a women. Amid bodies, souls, love is crystal clean white.

A longing of dogs is terrible. Silence too is just terrible...

DON'T ALLOW THAT WOMAN TO LEAVE...

The entire city was dressed with a woman flavor. A woman that is departing and has no clue where to go.
She just locked the door of her home. Departed alone with her interior dress and covered by a pink mantel. Underneath is found everything of her; all paths, all ups and downs, loves, farewells, victories and losses. And many unknown leaving from her...
A woman with long and dense hair. Where on every particle has thousands of others' lives, cards that were sent and not sent, wishes, longing and solitude.
The city was dressed with a woman aroma. A woman that is leaving, connected with the city of thousands of invisible particles. Men stop that woman! the pretty when getting out of the door, even if returning from longing, she is half foreign...

THE QUIET WORLD

The world has kept silence
A tongue is tied for an oak tree
where birds speak for other times
For waters occurs a possible invasion
A lazy Sun that goes up and down in a ritual
Winds that blow and hit old and new walls
For the love without love.

In a table of surgeons a soul is naked
New shapes of skulls and body parts
Unknown DNA from far away habitats
And somewhere a recently born baby from an exhausted vagina
Who does not know where is coming and where is going
Lost in road intersections without any memory.

The world is silent
In the refrain of its own song...

ALEPPO DEAD VICTIMS HAVE STARTED TO WALK

Alepo, dead victims have started to walk...
When the eye is pulsing we close our eye lids
Without asking what is far away
What stones were thrown and where did they fell
Arrow that burn the retina
The long entourage, coffee pots on fire
And for the longing of souls at night.

When we hear them calling by name
And we don't see anyone around
We answer confused and remain quiet
Without asking who has called us; the living and dead ones
And we succumb into a senseless fear
We urinate in a few minutes often and more often
And we brag
And we say: Evil!

But...Evil is nearby
There is no faster smell evaporating than blood
It pulls your eyelids and eye balls
And the one departing yesterday, is a breast fed kid
Sister and brother that took care of him, mother, father, cousin, neighbor
And others unknown

Because in Alepo dead bodies are starting to walk
For here and there
And we are quiet again
We cry for a moment when looking at those images
And then close our eyelids
Without asking for the eye ball pulled tomorrow

Because Evil is not far away
Evil is very close
And why not, also us...

MARRIED

The kid is awakened, cover him
To sing at the place and time that he is hiding from adults
And to wake up tomorrow when the Sun would wash the stones soil
The old man fell asleep, wake him up
To sit at the time and location that we, the youngsters used from him
And tomorrow the day would not complain, but to kiss the blurry view.
Me?! Marry myself with roads where steps jingle
As a ring in my finger place a tear of an oak tree.

...

From the end of a water well where I am now
As a soldier of no luck that measures time
With hours of Sun
I beg to jump up with a water made leash
A leash made of light
To return at the Oak tree, at the Eucalyptus, at the House Shade
To construct again my home from its foundation
To collect words sent from infinity of a sky
And over the soil the breath would uphold

It is better to hear thunders shaking the sky than listening to this silence.

Let dry trees to burn from lightning. In their place, forests and valleys full of flowers.

Unknown voices. Horses that are bursting in warm steam and begin their walk towards the creek.

Emptiness is death. Is overestimated, such a fall funeral.

Men, you are not leaves that fall so softly over a soil mudd...

CANDLE

Nothing has happened after you left
Nothing. Nothing.
In fact we were never together
We arrived alone at a time like a big dream
And you caused me, very much, very much pain.

Then I learned your secrets
We met each other
That hiding behind myself
When I had not met you
You sent them with a train of words
With kisses trapped under train racks.

I learned on how not to hate noisy trains
They do not wissle
Not even in my distant imagination
I counted the hits over my chest
I sent to you only butterflies
White and green butterflies.

Nothing has happened after your departure
Nothing. Nothing.
Candles that I lit were extinguished.
Only a candle of longing is on, hidden
The fire that distinguishes us, I want it to stay on
And keeps me pretty.

...

My love don't say anything
Don't say nothing
I was never awakened before the sun
To sit on the shade of an oak and pray for you
and then to relax above a morning dew
to kiss you entirely even by not staying there.

Don't say anything my love
don't say anything
I have never invited you before evening
To see each other through fire
But I built timid walls, filled of fear and anxiety
And awaited and waited to come through dreams
In silence, to extinguish my longing.

Don't say anything my love
Don't say anything
Let me speak non sense on my descend (deep, deep in solitude)
And to dodge a castle of sand
Now that I lost you
And you lost me!

WHO HAS JUST ARRIVED

Walls were applauding on their softness
With a dark rose from inside and opened from outside
Finally came the one whom I was waiting
A child that speaks all my languages
And I have in sync with her
As a sole watch running well
White shirts, cover the one who has just arrived
So that winds don't take him!

I have waited so much all my life
Oh! I have waited in the wooden door of luck
But the voice was descending as a piano melody
And was descending nearby a flower aroma
Away and far away,
Far and further away a smell was becoming attractive.

Applauds by walls of softness
The welcoming of one arriving recently
through depths of a dark rose,
Applauds and myself with a belated fate
The full voyage, liberated, infinitely far away...

...

I cannot get enough kisses with Sun. Perhaps because it is cold. Perhaps it is humid. Perhaps because people are escaping for somewhere. They are like frozen. They are like coming from far away. Hiding somewhere. From one another. Some from non sense and others from themselves.

I cannot get enough kisses from Sun; perhaps because of news that bring death notices ever more.

Dark ribbons on known and unknown profiles. As if trying to remind us that the majority on the other side are waiting for us. Birth and love are present anywhere but do not bother.

I cannot get enough from the Sun, I am hungry. Like earth at the end of a water well, where the Sun has never poured over it. But has engulfed its shoulders with darkness. Always waiting. Always waiting. a Deep and big kiss that would last forever. Ohhhh! I am not getting enough of this Sun, even this winter...

COLD...

Night. Cold. the City is tucked into its room. All doors are locked. and roads have closed gates. Fortunes are joking with breaths inside walls. painting the faces of those embodying it. There cannot be secrets at a smaller room. Because fortunes inside and outside are playing as they come.
Night. Cold. I am in a dead end. In search of a room. a Room with candles when hanging darkness. With a chimney on my front, where I can sit alone. To burn all that I don't have, that acts like it is. To abandon what I am deeply in a city of crazy men.
Since one day the crazy men will me mentioned once...

...

The kid is awakened cover him
To sing at the place and time that he is hiding from adults
And to wake up tomorrow when the Sun would wash the stones soil
The old man fell asleep, wake him up
To sit at the time and location that we, the youngsters used from him
And tomorrow the day would not complain, but to kiss the blurry view.
Me?! Marry myself with roads where steps jingle
As a ring in my finger place a tear of an oak tree.

...

From the end of a water well where I am know
As a soldier of no luck that measures time
with hours of Sun
I beg to jump up with a water made leash
A leash made of light
To return at the Oak tree, at the Eucalyptus, at the House Shade
To construct again my home from its foundation
To collect words sent from infinity of a sky
And over the soil the breath would uphold.

...

It is better to hear thunders shaking the sky than listening to this silence.
Let dry trees to burn from lightning. In their place, forests and valleys full of flowers. And Unknown voices. Horses that are bursting in warm steam and begin their walk towards the creek.
Emptiness is death. Is overestimated, such a fall funeral. Men, you are not leaves that fall so softly over a soil mudd...

...

My love don't say anything
Don't say nothing
I was never awakened before the sun
To sit on the shade of an oak tree and pray for you
and then to relax above a morning dew
to kiss you entirely even by not staying there.

Don't say anything my love
don't say anything
I have never invited you before evening
To see each other through fire
But I built timid walls, filled of fear and anxiety
And awaited and waited to come through dreams
In silence, to extinguish my longing.

Don't say anything my love
Don't say anything
Let me speak non sense on my descend (deep, deep in solitude)
And to dodge a castle of sand
Now that I lost you
And you lost me!

WHO HAS JUST ARRIVED

Walls were applauding on their softness
With a dark rose from inside and opened from outside
Finally came the one whom I was waiting
A child that speaks all my languages
And I have in sync with her
As a sole watch running well
White shirts, cover the one who has just arrived
So that winds don't take him!

I have waited so much all my life
Oh! I have waited in the wooden door of luck
But the voice was descending as a piano melody
And was descending nearby a flower aroma
Away and far away,
Far and further away a smell was becoming attractive.

Applauds by walls of softness
The welcoming of one arriving recently
through depths of a dark rose,
Applauds and myself with a belated fate
The full voyage, liberated, infinitely far away...

COLD...

Night. Cold. the City is tucked into its room. All doors are locked. and roads have closed gates. Fortunes are joking with breaths inside walls. painting the faces of those embodying it. There cannot be secrets at a smaller room. Because fortunes inside and outside are playing as they come.
Night. Cold. I am in a dead end. In search of a room. a Room with candles when hanging darkness. With a chimney on my front, where I can sit alone. To burn all that I don't have, that acts like it is. To abandon what I have deeply seen in a city of crazy men.
Since one day the crazy men will be mentioned once ...

...

Men is a perfect home. Constructed by meat, blood, copper, stone, wood, water and air. There is so much light inside him. There are also dirty, dark corners where mysterious matters blow. is the only home sensitive, with all its breathing pores. The only, the only. Think of a home always on the move. Awakened, sleeping and in death.

Again, it is the only one, only one, the only one. A home were all colors are found. A home will all particular voices. Where love and hate are its anthem. Where edges contain all weight. Where perfection is tear and smile. Where a frightening feeling is a measure of darkness.

...

Try to enter on one of the edges, and you will feel a sense of destruction. At times impossible to return at the first state of mind. In that unique construction, where all those making the so called home, keep alive each other. And where each one of them are walls, basement, at times are a roof and at times are voices.
Where the home foundation is a mystery in itself.
...
Ourselves is all this home. The Difference is simply the window that we open; the one where light or evil enters. ...

Much time passed to loose your soul inside myself. Prayers only keep away prayers ... But at the end the soul. You died of unfinished life. (There are these sort of departures). In one of its halves, hair is taller and taller. Has a green color. The announcement of department is the Sun's dawn. And the Sun of this Summer is completely sad. ...

Oh! The greatest history of shadows of these leaves standing on our walls, and water is purer than dreams, recognition, recognition that all this is not a dream!
My soul is chocking from deception like a worried sea unraveling its stress. A strong wind is felt around myself. And suspicion falls over the realities of matters.

WHY

But if someone is not satisfied with his own sadness, let him make it public! And I think that he should be killed, otherwise, rebellion will unravel....
WHY
Why are you upset for the Sun that traveled far away and has stopped somewhere else. And struggling sadly to know about what he is doing and who is with him. Why are you killing the time with a hat in winter.

How do you know that Sun's trip and his presence somewhere else is not more struggling than our solitude. How do you know that he is not longing for not being able to come back.

Come on be happy from an ego inside the a dark grey, with which you grab yourself. Everyone call deeply on the ego when succumbing into sadness. Because, like anyone else, you are wrong.

You forget that inside yourself the Sun is greater than the one departing to somewhere else whose rays are needed by anyone.
Tell me why are you sad, since you are the Sun that walks.
Tell me...

All of my dead items are playing music and dancing. A unique spectacle, that begun at noon. That is the way to pay, I am sitting at the brightest spot of the house.
And I see myself on all its shapes, as if my items were alive. On no one separately, but not on all of them, I am not in my entirety.
As a result there are present my own dead items and are dancing. They are telling me that their departure was an obligation. New items are coming towards myself.

...

My WATCH is much crazy than myself. She is turned on every time she pleases. Moves on the opposite directions. Sometimes I ask her for a cherry flower, she brings me a blackberry.

I ask her to play a guitar, she plays a bell in a church, when no one is there. I request a wooden home in the middle of a forest or at the shores of a lake, she abandoned me at a time when dogs are complaining for not hearing their own barking.
I tell her go to hell, she doesn't go any way. She reminds me of the cordon of a belly button. Shouldn't I break the head of my watch?

A ROSE

If the World would not be so naive and superficial
To have the eyes to succumb inside yourself only one
instant and to touch your upper lips,

To listen to your language of silence and to fair through the
soul where colors are breaking borders among themselves,
As if the World would have time and not handle greater
challenges and
smaller than herself,
But one instant, only one instant to see you
Very pretty, sweet, humble and pristine
Then he would not fair through the mysteries and turmoil
of winds
Because you are testimony of breadth and divine love, A
ROSE ...

SHORT BIOGRAPHY – Trëndafile Visha

Trëndafile Visha was born in the city of Kolesian, Kukës on 12.6.1966. She completed her studies at the High Institute of Agriculture of Kamëz, Tirana. For nearly 20 years she has worked in print media, initially for "Shekulli" newspaper and 16 years for "Gazeta Shqiptare". In November 2016 Visha published the book of poetry "I've stolen my eyes" and the book of meditations (poetry and poetic prose): "The same luck in 100 journeys".

SHORT BIOGRAPHY – Peter Tase

Peter Tase was born and grown in Albania (1982), moved with his family to the United States in 2000 and graduated from Whitefish Bay High School (Wisconsin), in 2001. In December - 2006 received a Bachelor of Arts Degree in Italian Literature and Political Sciences from University of Wisconsin – Milwaukee. In spring, 2006, studied at the Les Aspin Center for Government (Marquette University), in Washington DC, his research focused on US Government, International Affairs and Geopolitics. In 2005 Tase worked for *Whyte Hirschboeck Dudek* SC in Milwaukee (WI) as a Telecommunications Law Research Associate. In 2007 – 2009 worked for the U.S. Peace Corps in South America and implemented a variety of projects on International Sustainable Development (Public Health, Civil Engineering and Education). In August, 2012 Peter started working as International Programs Assistant, for the Secretariat of International Federation of Engineering Education Societies (IFEES) and Global Engineering Deans Council (GEDC). During his tenure at the GEDC (under the guidance of Executive Secretary) he was able to establish academic connections between GEDC leadership and two universities in Bosnia and Herzegovina. Peter worked full time for IFEES and GEDC until January 2015. Over the last three years he is working as a consultant to secretariat of both organizations (IFEES/GEDC) focused on matters of international affairs. Since 2015 he has consulted various U.S. Universities (IIT Chicago – Kent College of Law, Augsburg University and University of Wisconsin - Milwaukee) as well as foreign governments (Albania, Azerbaijan, Bosnia and Herzegovina, Kosovo) on issues pertaining to: globalization of tertiary education, international trade, government transparency and public policies that harness intercultural dialogue. He has published many articles and papers on: the

Caucasus Region, the Balkan Peninsula, integration of South East European countries into the European Union and current affairs in Turkey and Syria. Peter Tase has translated into English and Spanish over twenty poetry volumes from over 15 Albanian writers and authors. His entire work, including research and journalism, is constantly published in the United States, Latin America, Vietnam and Europe.

www.ingramcontent.com/pod-product-compliance
Lightning Source LLC
Chambersburg PA
CBHW031439040426

42444CB00006B/894